MAKING
Bread

MAKING
Bread

RUTH THOMSON
PHOTOGRAPHY: CHRIS FAIRCLOUGH

FRANKLIN WATTS

LONDON/NEW YORK/SYDNEY/TORONTO

Franklin Watts
12a Golden Square
London W1R 4BA

Franklin Watts Australia
14 Mars Road
Lane Cove
N.S.W. 2066

Copyright © 1986 Franklin Watts

ISBN: 0 86 313 429 7

Design: Edward Kinsey

Illustrations: Kathleen McDougall

Printed in Belgium

The publisher, author and
photographer would like to
thank Aubrey Karn of Fieldside
Bakery, Elstead for his help in
the preparation of this book.

CONTENTS

TAKE A CLOSER LOOK

Bread is one of our most important foods and also one of the oldest foods known. You probably eat it as part of every meal.

Think of all the dozens of kinds of loaves there are to choose from. White loaves include farmhouse, cob, cottage, tin, bloomer, barrel, French stick, cob, plait, Danish or Coburg. There are brown and wholemeal breads, milk, fruit, malt, cheese and soda breads. There are rolls, baps, buns, croissants and muffins. Can you think of any others?

▽ Bread is a nourishing food, which provides us with energy, protein, minerals and fibre.

Whatever its shape, size and colour, the basic ingredients of bread are the same. Flour, yeast, salt, fat and water are mixed together to form a dough, which is then shaped and baked.

Most bakers use flour made from wheat grain, which is ground into a fine powder. In some parts of the world, people also grind the grain of rye, maize or sorghum to make flour.

The yeast makes the bread light and airy. It is a living plant which, when mixed with warm water, makes bubbles of gas. This gas makes the bread rise. In India, parts of Africa and the Middle East, people eat flat, or unleavened, bread which does not contain yeast. It is dense and heavy.

△ The basic ingredients for bread are 1. salt and fat 2. yeast 3. water 4. flour.

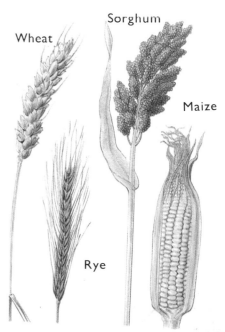

Wheat

Sorghum

Maize

Rye

MAKING THE DOUGH

◁ Sacks of flour are kept in a storeroom above the bakery. Flour is tipped down a huge funnel into a mixing bowl below.

▽ Mr Karn buys fresh yeast each week and keeps it refrigerated until he needs to use it.

Mr Karn has been a village baker for over forty years. Each weekday, he is up at 4.30 am to bake the day's batch of bread and cakes. On Saturdays, when there is extra demand, he starts work at 1.30 am.

To save time in the mornings, Mr Karn measures out the flour for the next day's baking in the afternoon before. He pours it down a chute, straight into a dough mixer. He adds measured amounts of salt and fat. The following morning, he weighs the yeast and crumbles it into tiny pieces.

Finally, he adds water to the bowl, after whisking the yeast into it. The temperature of the water he uses depends upon the weather. In hot weather, he uses water straight from the cold tap. In cold weather, warm water is used instead.

When the machine is turned on, the dough hook turns round and round, mixing the ingredients into a smooth, soft dough. This takes about ten minutes.

Mr Karn stops the machine once to feel the dough. He can tell, by experience, whether he needs to add more water to the mixture. He scrapes the sides of the bowl to stop the dough from sticking.

Once the dough is mixed, it is left for an hour, while the yeast starts to work.

△ Water is measured out into a bucket.

◁ A huge machine mixes the flour, yeast, salt, fat and water.

▷ When the dough is fully mixed, it can be easily carried. Notice the end of the flour chute above Mr Karn's head.

The minute cells of yeast start to give off bubbles of carbon dioxide gas, which make the dough expand. Mr Karn puts a thermometer into the dough. The temperature of the dough rises as the yeast does its work. After an hour, it has risen to 78°.

Mr Karn cuts pieces which are the right weight to make a loaf. By law, finished loaves must weigh a certain weight, according to their size. A weights and measures inspector makes regular visits to bakeries, to check that loaves are the correct weight for their size.

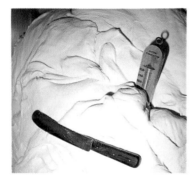

△ A thermometer is pushed into the dough to measure its temperature.

▷ The dough is cut into different size pieces according to the type of bread to be made.

Because Mr Karn is an experienced baker, he can cut pieces that are virtually the right weight. All the same, he puts each piece on the scales to check its weight and adds or removes a bit of dough when necessary.

The amount of dough cut for each loaf is heavier than the eventual weight of the finished loaf. This is because a loaf loses weight during baking, as the moisture in it is driven off by the heat of the oven. To make a finished loaf weighing 800 g, Mr Karn cuts a piece of dough that weighs 950 g.

△ The dough for a loaf must weigh exactly the right amount.

13

◁ The dough is kneaded into balls using the heel of the hand.

Mr Karn kneads some of the pieces, by hand, into balls. Kneading breaks any enormous gas bubbles in the dough, which might otherwise leave big holes when the bread is baked. This is called handing-up.

He puts the balls, quite widely spaced, on a floured wooden tray and covers them with a cotton cloth. The cloth helps both to keep the dough warm (since yeast can only work in the warm) and to prevent a skin from forming on the outside of the balls.

The dough is left to rise. This process is called proving. Once the dough has proved, it is ready to be shaped into loaves.

▽ The dough is covered with a cloth and left for about an hour to rise.

SHAPING THE DOUGH

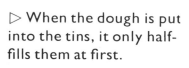
◁ The risen dough is dropped into a machine which moulds it into long sausages.

Dough for making tin and sandwich loaves is shaped in an automatic moulding machine. Mr Karn drops a piece of dough into a feeder at the top of the machine. The dough is carried on a conveyor belt between moving rollers. These squash and shape it into a long flat sausage, which drops into a trough.

Mr Karn puts each sausage into a greased loaf tin. He covers the tins with a cotton cloth and leaves the dough to prove yet again.

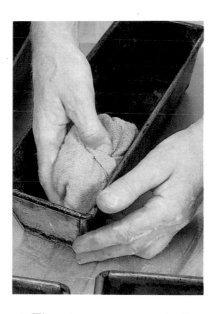

△ The tins are greased all over with oil.

▷ When the dough is put into the tins, it only half-fills them at first.

▷ Cottage loaves are hand-moulded. Mr Karn divides a ball of dough so that one piece is twice as big as the other. He rolls them both into balls. He flattens the top of the larger one and presses the smaller ball on top. He makes a deep hole in the top with his thumb and cuts slashes all the way round both pieces.

▷ Plaits are hand-moulded as well. Mr Karn splits a ball into three equal sized pieces and rolls them into long sticks. He then plaits these sticks, just as you might plait wool or hair, pressing them together at the ends. Finally, he sprinkles poppyseed over the top for decoration.

◁ Bloomers are moulded by machine but Mr Karn has to give them a final moulding by hand. He cuts several slashes across the top before baking, so that the loaves will 'bloom' or rise better. Since they are not baked in tins, the loaves have a crispy crust all over.

▽ Dough is made into many shapes and sizes.

WHOLEMEAL AND BROWN BREAD

Germ

Endosperm

Bran

▽ Brown bread dough is much coarser in texture than white bread dough.

Mr Karn does not make only white bread, he also makes wholemeal and brown bread, using different types of flour.

Wholemeal flour is made by grinding the whole wheatgrain. This is made up of the bran (the skin), the germ (the part from which a new plant will grow) and the endosperm (the inside). Wholemeal flour is the most nutritious kind of flour because none of the goodness of the grain is lost in milling.

Brown flour is made with all the endosperm, but only some of the bran and germ.

White flour is made entirely from the endosperm. Vitamins and minerals are often added to it to make up for what has been lost in milling.

Wholemeal and brown dough are made in a similar way to white dough but the look and the texture differ.

▽ The dough must also be kneaded before being put into tins and allowed to rise.

BAKING THE BREAD

After an hour or so, the dough has risen right to the top of the tins. The loaves are now ready to be baked.

Sandwich loaf tins have a lid on them. This helps to make the shape of the finished loaves as square as possible and ensures that the top of the loaves does not become too brown and crispy during baking. Mr Karn slashes the tops of the other tin loaves with a sharp knife.

He puts the tins into the oven with a long-handled wooden tool called a peel.

▷ The tins are packed into an oven which has three separate compartments.

▽ The dough more than doubles its size in the tins during the rising process.

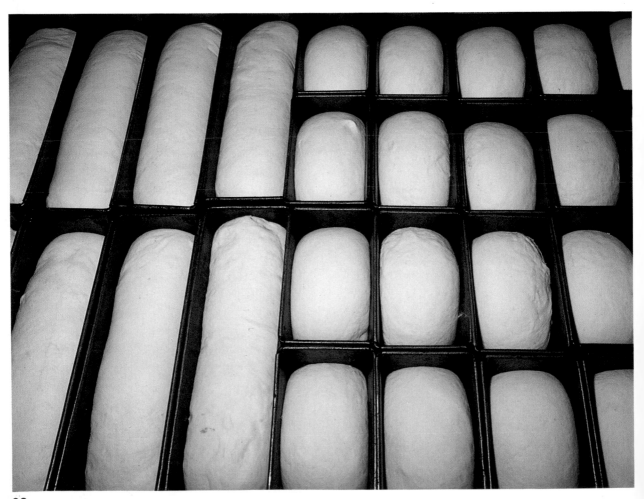

◁ The tins are lifted out of the oven two at a time.

The loaves are baked for about forty minutes. As the heat of the oven cooks the dough, so it also kills the yeast and drives off the bubbles of gas. However, the tiny holes where the gas was remain. If you look closely at a slice of bread, you will see them.

When the loaves are ready, Mr Karn lifts the trays and tins out with the peel. He tips the loaves into a wire tray to cool. He stacks the tins upside-down in a pile.

Now you can see why tin loaves are crispy and browned only on the top and not on the sides.

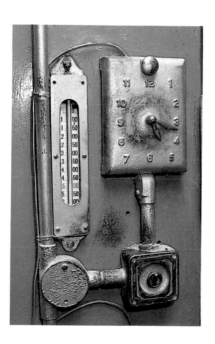

△ A thermometer shows the temperature of the oven, which is usually between 450–475°F. A clock shows the time when the bread will be ready.

▷ Putting the loaves into a wire tray allows them to cool on all sides at once.

25

△ Many types of loaves including cottage loaves and bloomers are also baked on flat trays.

◁ Sandwich rolls are baked in tins with lids.

▷ Rolls are baked on flat trays.

READY FOR SALE

◁ The bread is arranged on the shelves according to its size and type.

The trays of bread are wheeled straight from the bakery into the shop. Mr Karn times his baking with great precision, so that the first batch of bread is ready at 8.30 am, when the shop opens.

His work for the day is not over. For the rest of the morning he will bake more bread, cakes, rolls and any special orders. He will clean the bakery so that it is spotless, grease the baking tins and measure out the flour for tomorrow.

Mr Karn enjoys his work. He says there is always something new to learn and that each day's baking is different.

▽ White loaves are usually the most popular type of bread.

THE PROCESS AT A GLANCE

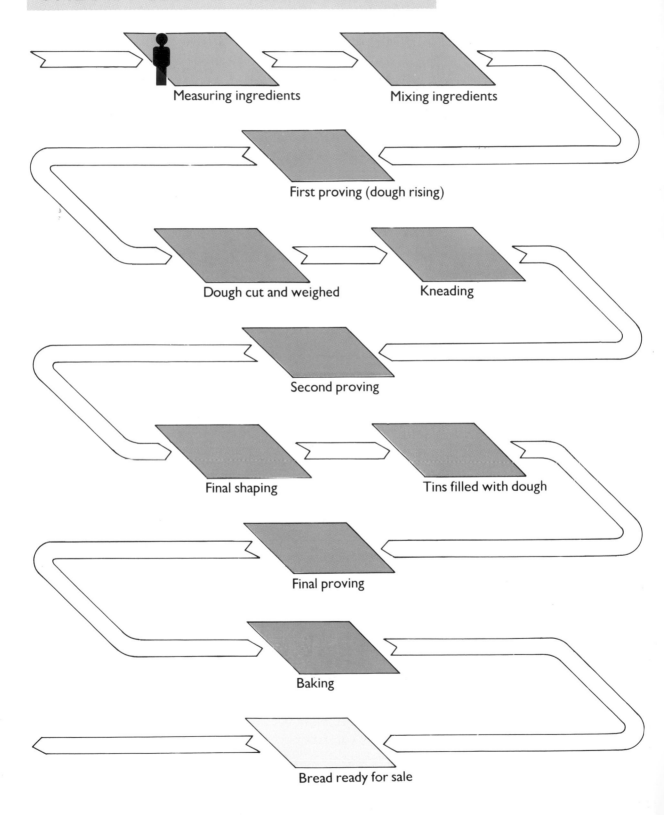

Measuring ingredients

Mixing ingredients

First proving (dough rising)

Dough cut and weighed

Kneading

Second proving

Final shaping

Tins filled with dough

Final proving

Baking

Bread ready for sale

FACTS ABOUT BREAD

Bread has been a main source of food for man for at least 5,000 years. The ancient Egyptians discovered yeast and began baking risen loaves. The ancient Romans brought better methods of milling flour and bread-making to Britain.

Bread today provides about 14% of the total energy and protein needs of the British people. Around 10 million loaves are eaten everyday which is 6% of all British food production. Every year about £2,000 million is spent on bread in Britain.

More than 80% of the wheat used in British bread-making is grown in the United Kingdom.

The British baking industry is highly automated and employs about 10,000 people.

White bread accounts for about 68% of all bread sales. Brown and wholemeal breads have about 19% of sales. The remaining 13% is made on speciality breads such as fruit, or malt loaves and rolls. Brown and wholemeal breads are gaining in popularity.

Some types of bread

Sandwich loaf. Has a flat top giving even, square slices and may be white or brown. A small loaf gives 10–12 slices; a large loaf 20–24 slices.

Barrel. Baked in a corrugated, hinged tin to give a fluted cylindrical shape.

Danish. Open baked loaf with a heavy dusting of flour and with one deep cut across the top.

Bloomer. Long loaf with rounded ends. The top is slashed several times before baking so that the loaf can 'bloom' up or rise better.

Cob. A round loaf which can have a sprinkling of crushed wheat on top.

Coburg. A dome shaped loaf baked on the oven bottom.

Cottage. A traditional, hand made bread, baked on the oven bottom. It is easily recognisable with its two round pieces.

Long split tin. Given a deep cut down the centre before baking. Popular because of the many handy slices into which it can be cut.

French stick. Long thin baton, thick crisp crust with or without poppy seeds, at its best a few hours after baking.

Poppy seed plait. Very crusty plaited loaf decorated with poppy seeds.

Farmhouse. Baked in a tin with the rounded corners, dusted with flour and cut down the centre before baking.

Flat loaves (Baps). These loaves are known by traditional names in different regions e.g. Scotch bap, Irish bap, Devon flat, Essex paddle.

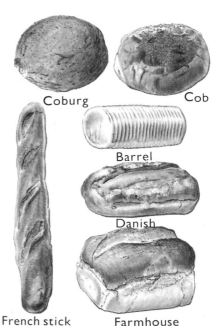

Coburg Cob

Barrel

Danish

French stick Farmhouse

INDEX

PRINTED IN BELGIUM BY
proost
INTERNATIONAL BOOK PRODUCTION